Guitar/Vocal

Classic
JAMES TAYLOR

MW00804908

...ncludes Complete Solos

Contents

Transcribed and Arranged by SCOTT HATHAWAY

"Flag"
© 1979 CBS Inc.

"James Taylor" album cover photo: Norman Seeff
© 1976 Warner Bros. Records Inc.

"One Man Dog" album cover photo: Peter Simon
© 1972 Warner Bros. Records Inc.

"Sweet Baby James" album cover photo: Henry Diltz

Guitar Works, Inc.
3335 West Cary Street
Richmond, Virginia 23221
804-358-0855
www.guitarworksinc.com

Don't Let Me Be Lonely Tonight

Words and Music by
JAMES TAYLOR

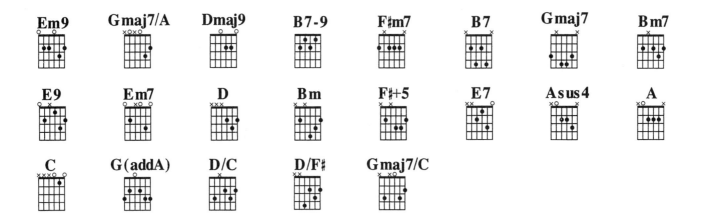

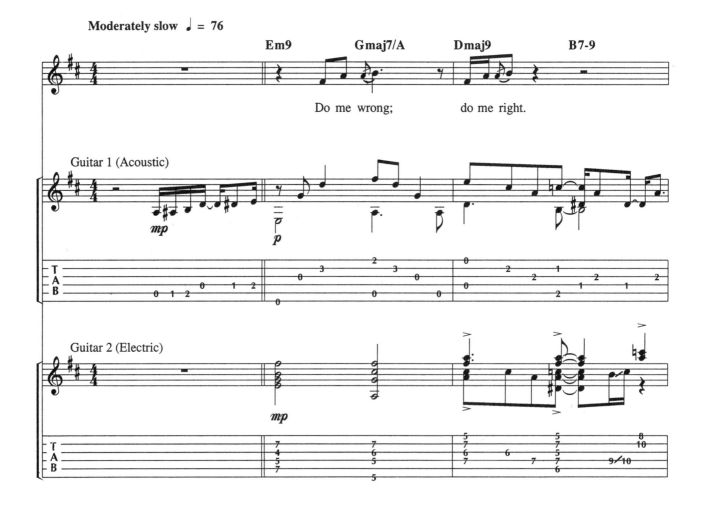

Tell me lies,— but hold— me tight.— Save your good-byes for— the morn-

ing light,— but don't let me be lone - ly to - night.—

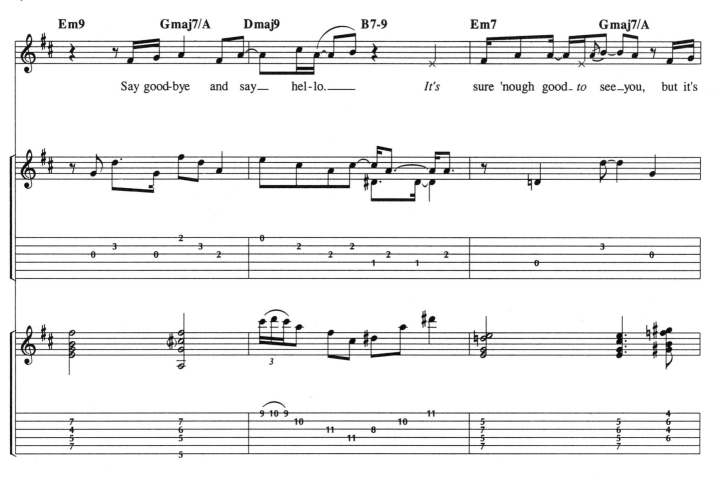

Say good-bye and say— hel-lo.—— *It's* sure 'nough good— *to* see— you, but it's

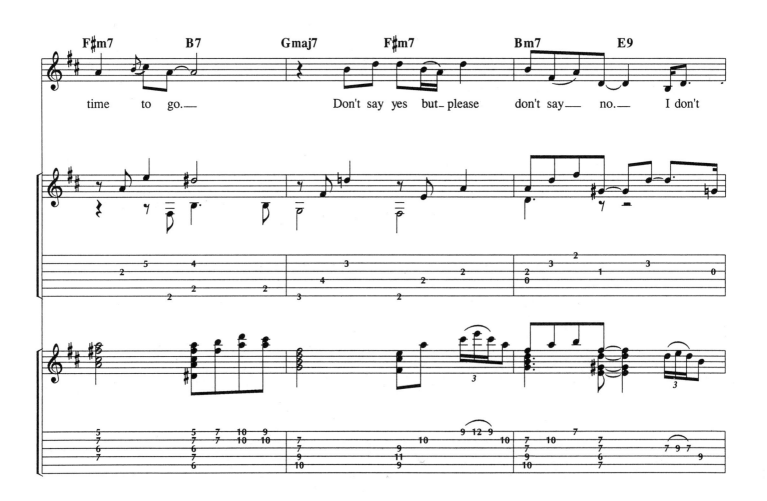

time to go.— Don't say yes but— please don't say— no.— I don't

want to be lone-ly to-night.___ Go a-way then damn___ ya. Go on___

and___ do as you please____ yea,. now. You ain't gon-na see me___ get-tin' down on my knees.___

I'm un-de-cid-ed and your heart's been di-vid-ed. You've been turn-ing my world up-side

down, no, no. So do me wrong;

do me right,- right now_ ba - by.   Go on and tell me lies   but hold   me tight.___

Save your good-byes for the morn - in' light morn-in' light,_ but don't   let me be lone-ly to-night.

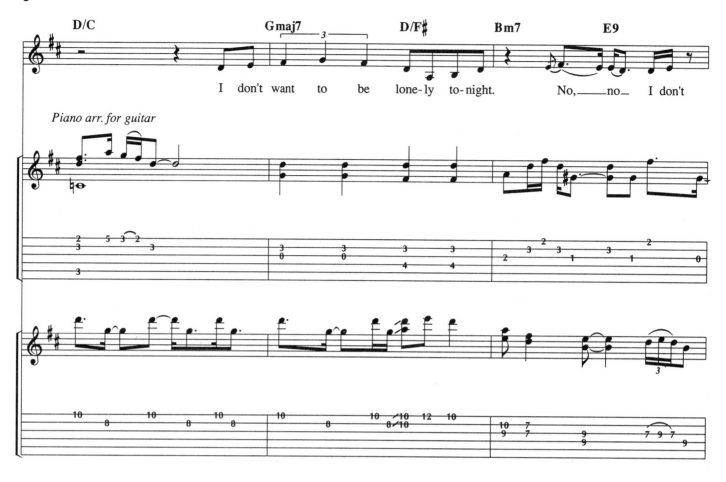

I don't want to be lone-ly to-night. No,——no— I don't

want to— be lone-ly to-night.—

Fire And Rain

Words and Music by
JAMES TAYLOR

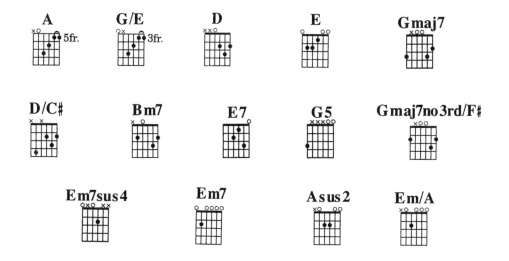

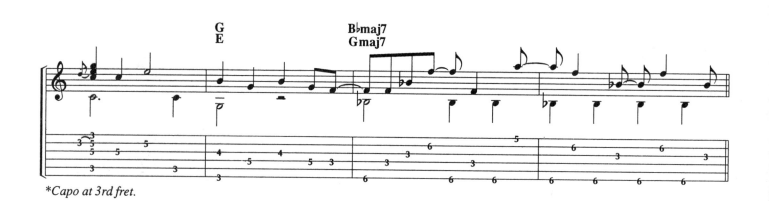

*Capo at 3rd fret.

I've seen___ lone-ly times___ when I could___
_ not___ find_ a friend._
But I al-ways thought_that I'd
see you___ a-gain.

With Fill 2, 2nd time.

Fill 2
Guitar

Guitar maintains "Asus2" until fade. (Without capo Csus2)

Long Ago And Far Away

Words and Music by
JAMES TAYLOR

*Capo at 2nd fret.

Up On The Roof

Words and Music by
GERRY GOFFIN and CAROLE KING

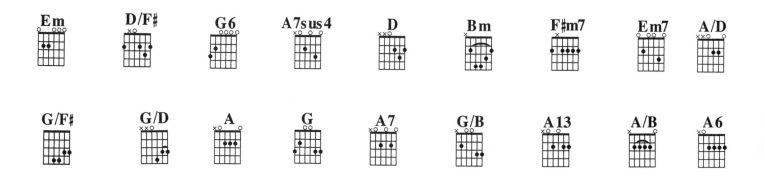

*Capo at 3rd fret.

*No capo

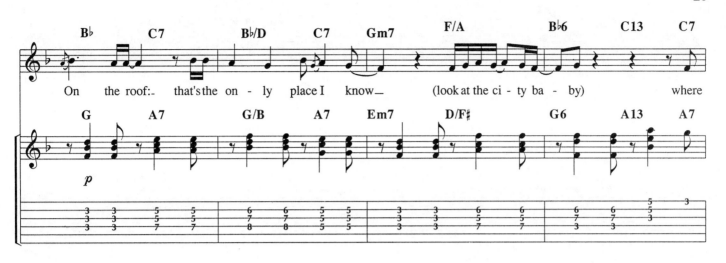

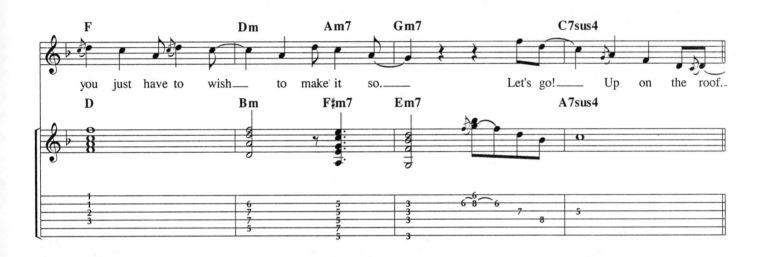

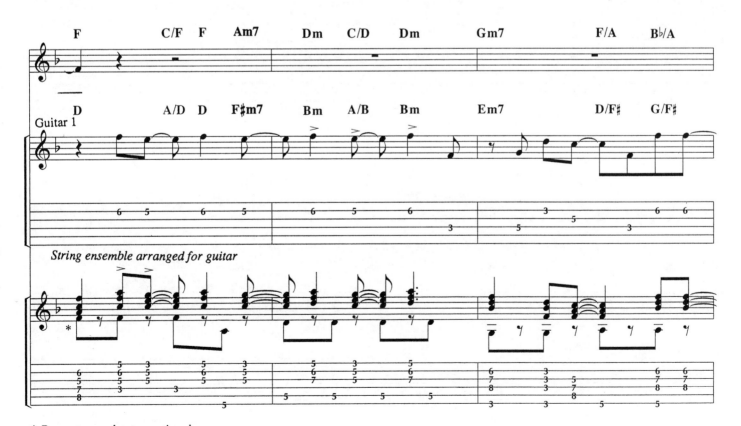

Downstemmed notes optional.

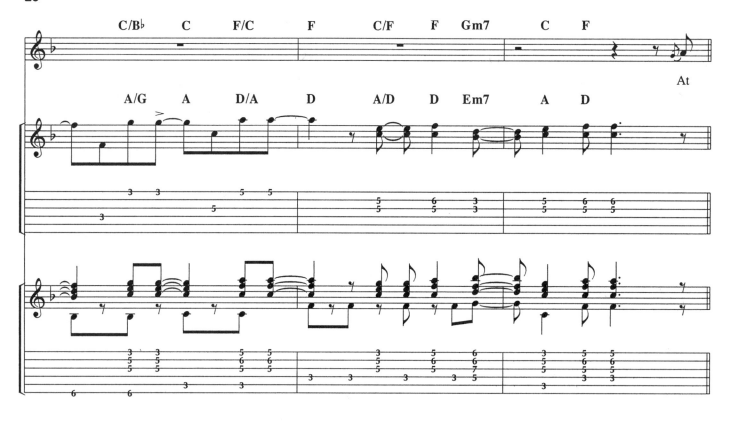

At

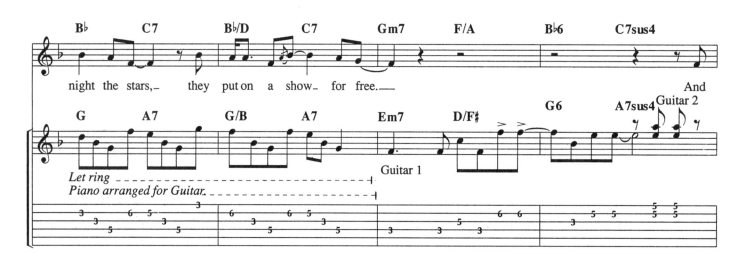

night the stars,— they put on a show— for free.—

And

Let ring -

Piano arranged for Guitar. - - - - - - - - - - - -

Guitar 1

Guitar 2

dar - ling, you can share———— it all— with me.——

That's what I

said. Keep on tel- ling you that right smack dab___ in the mid- dle of___ town,   I

found   a   par - a - dise___   that's trou - ble   proof.___

With Fill 1

And   if this old world   start's a   get- ting you___ down,   there's

Guitars 1 and 2

** *Implied by Keyboard.*
* *Implied by Bass.*

Fill 1
Guitar 3

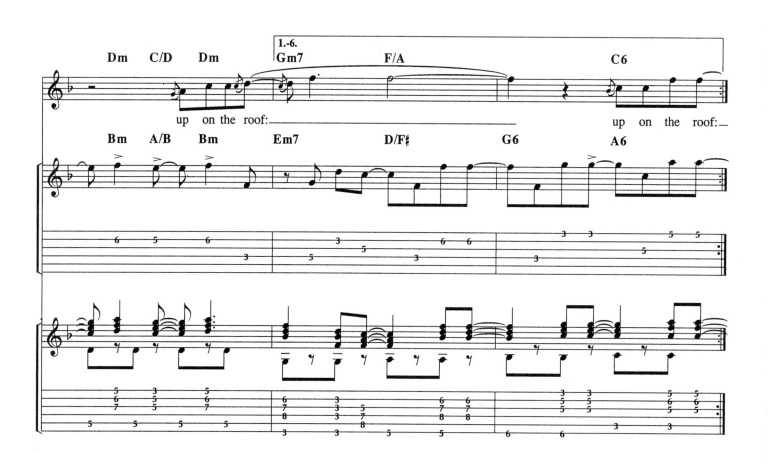

Additional Lyrics

Everything is alright.
Everything is alright.
Come on, drop what you're
doing tonight and climb
up the stairs.

We got the stars above,
and the city lights below,
ooh, up on a roof, now.

YOUR SMILING FACE

Words and Music by
JAMES TAYLOR

Carolina In My Mind

Words and Music by
JAMES TAYLOR

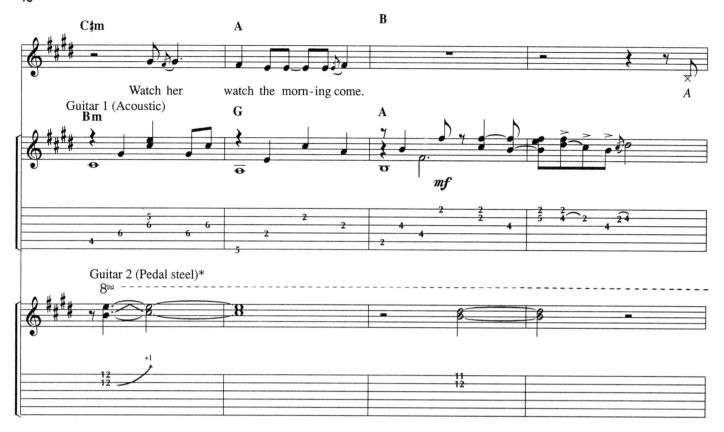

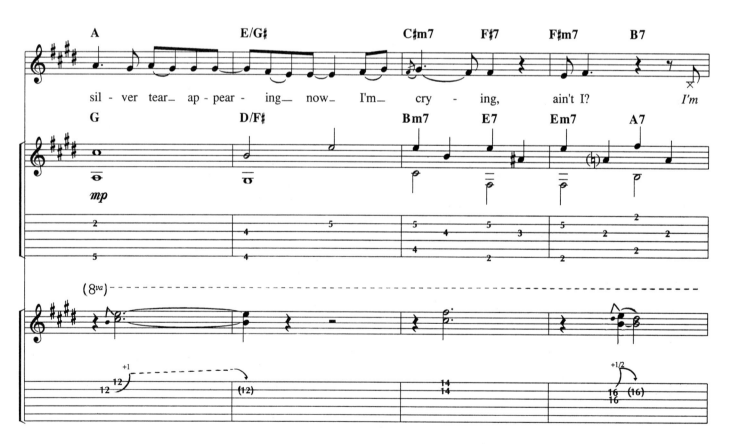

*Arranged for Guitar

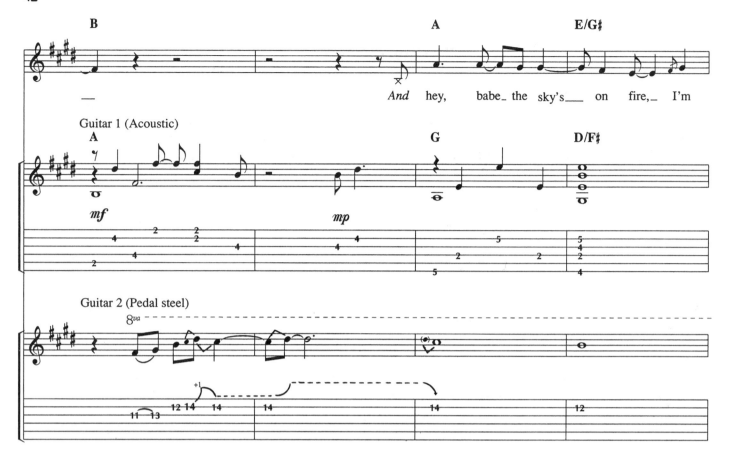

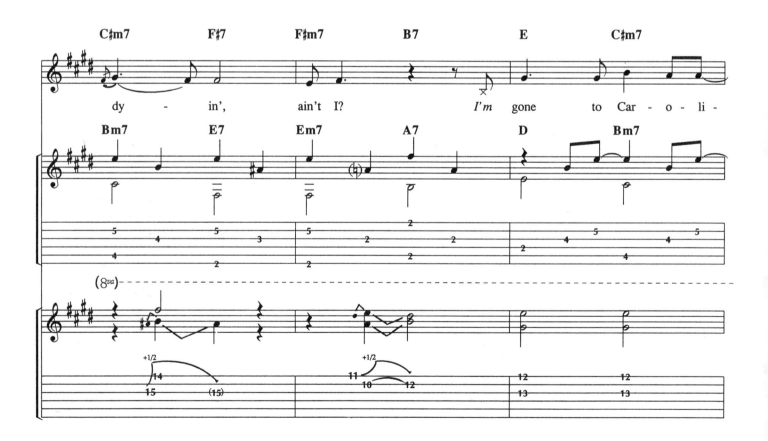

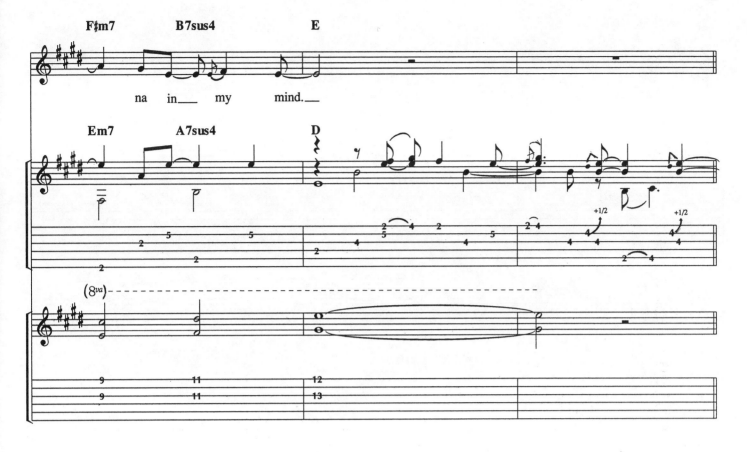

na in___ my mind.___

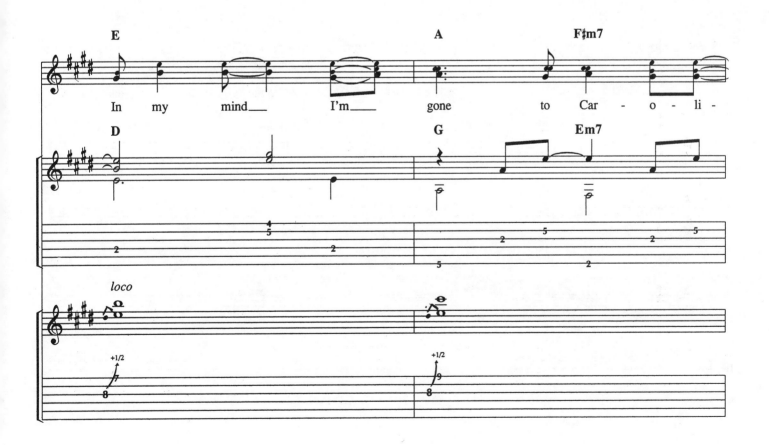

In my mind___ I'm___ gone to Car - o - li -

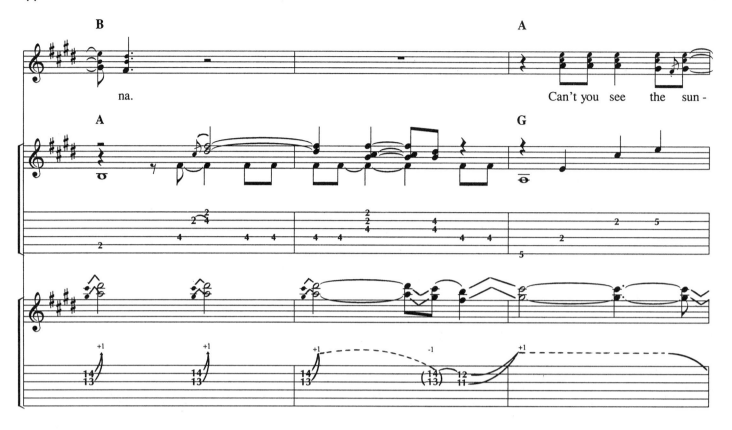

na.
Can't you see the sun-

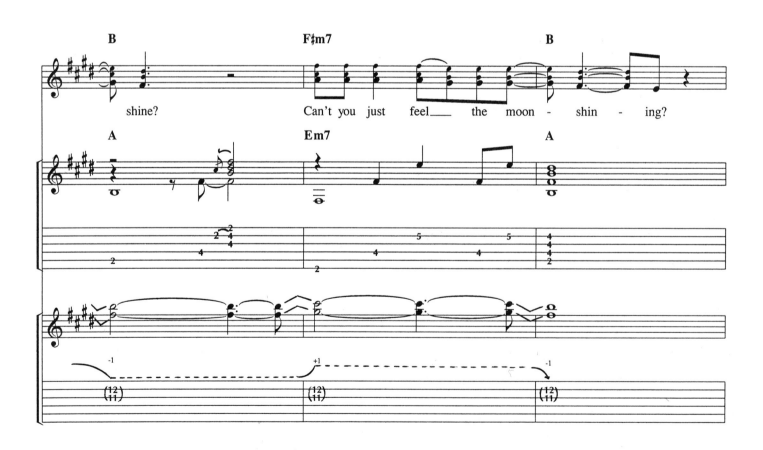

shine?
Can't you just feel____ the moon - shin - ing?

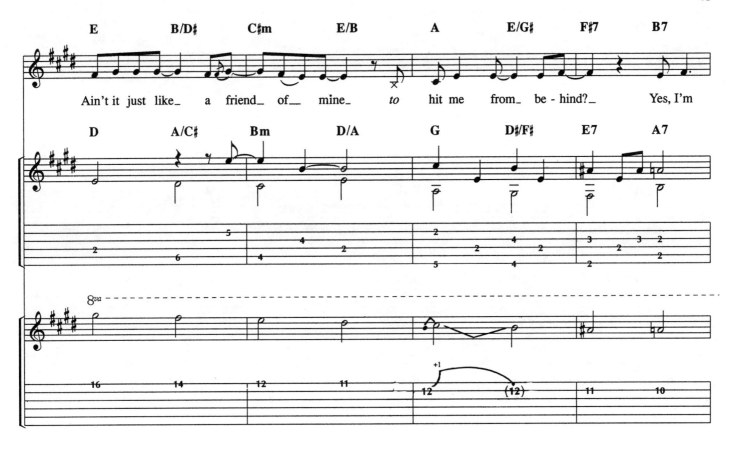

Ain't it just like_ a friend_ of_ mine_ *to* hit me from_ be - hind?_ Yes, I'm

gone to Car - o - li - na in_ my mind._

me, still I'm on__ the dark__ side of__ the moon.__

And it seems__ like it goes on like this for-ev-

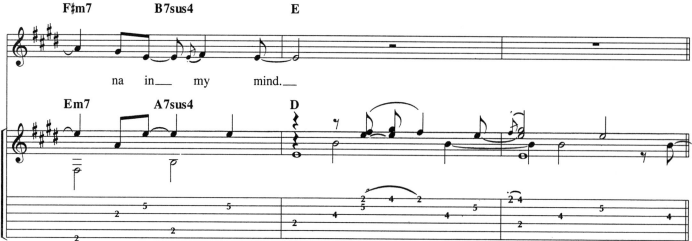

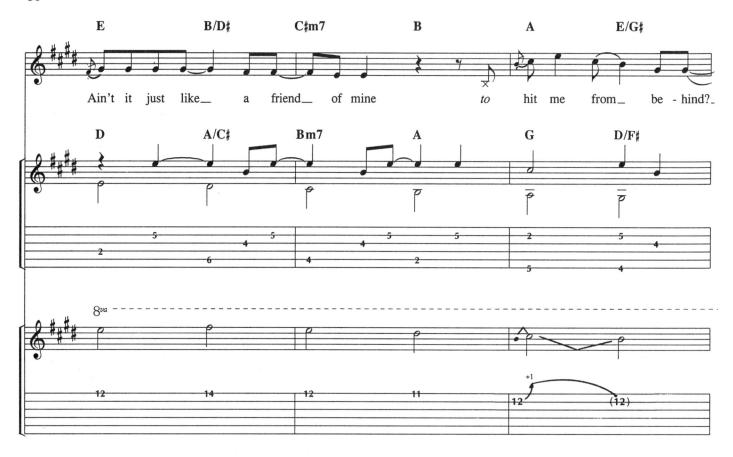

Ain't it just like__ a friend__ of mine *to* hit me from__ be - hind?__

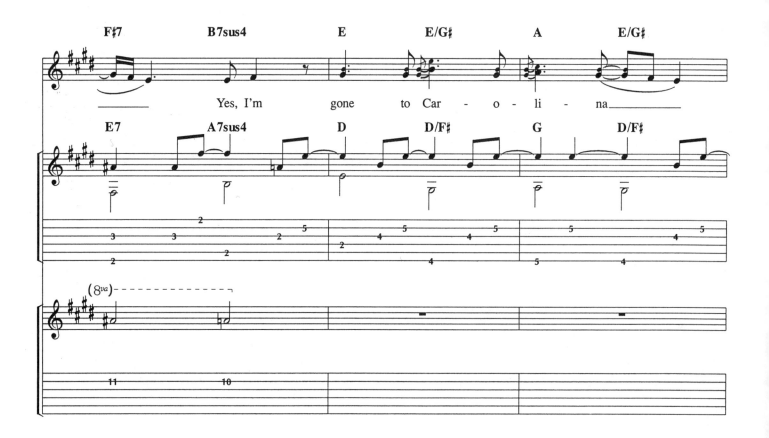

Yes, I'm gone to Car - o - li - na_____

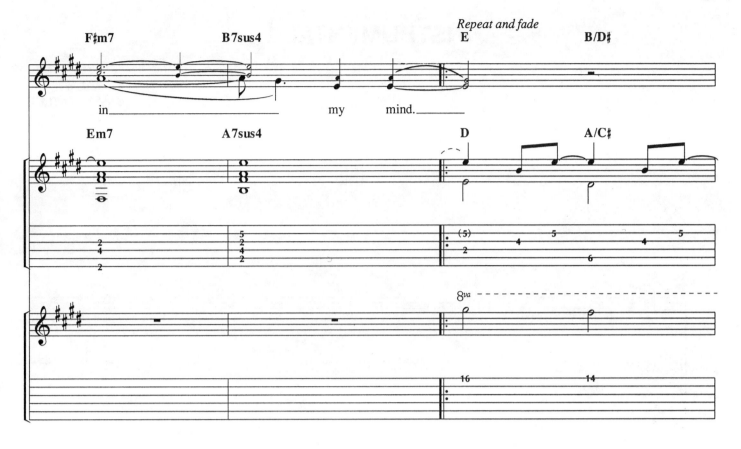

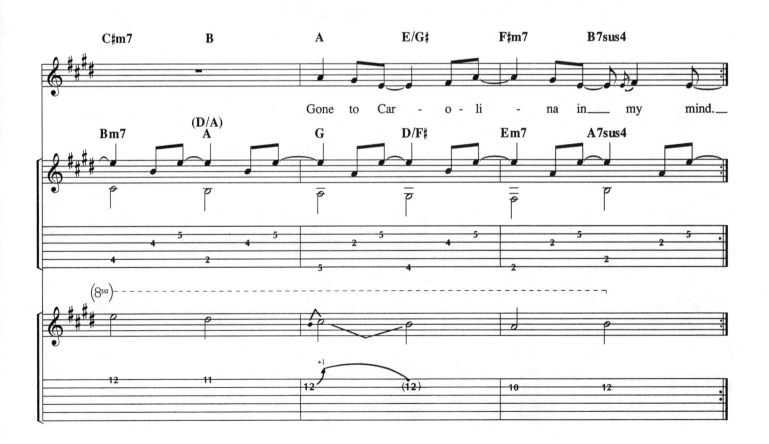

INSTRUMENTAL I

Music by
JAMES TAYLOR

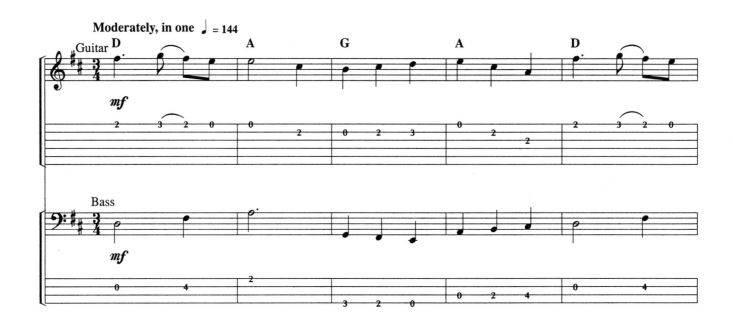

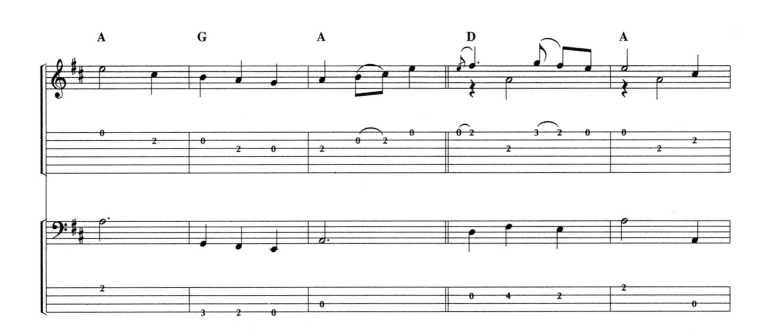

INSTRUMENTAL II

Music by
JAMES TAYLOR

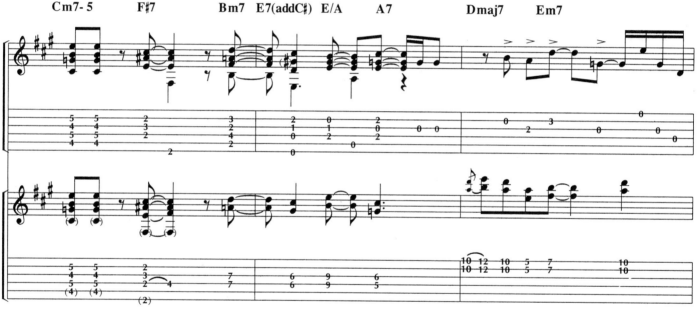

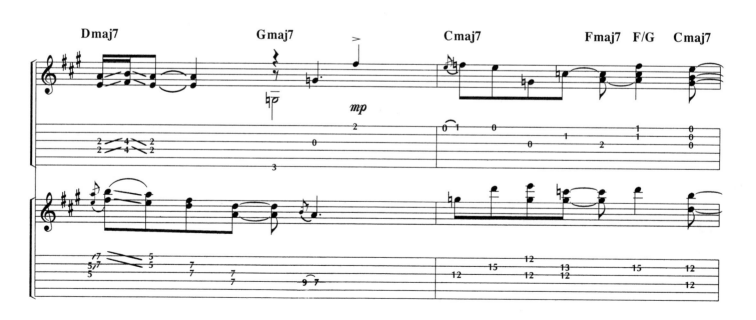

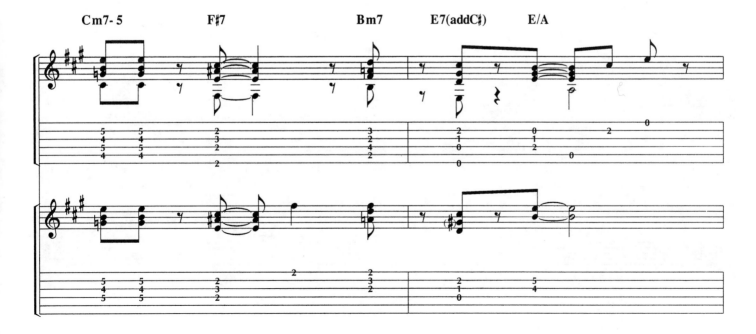

Country Road

Words and Music by
JAMES TAYLOR

*Guitar 1
legato

Take to the high - way won't you lend me— your— name?—

*Tune 6 string to D

Mexico

Words and Music by
JAMES TAYLOR

Capo at 2nd fret. Two acoustic guitars arranged as one.

Shower The People

Words and Music by
JAMES TAYLOR

You can play the game and you can act out the part, though you

know it was-n't writ-ten for you. *But* tell me how you can stand there with your

*Capo at 3rd fret.

Chorus:

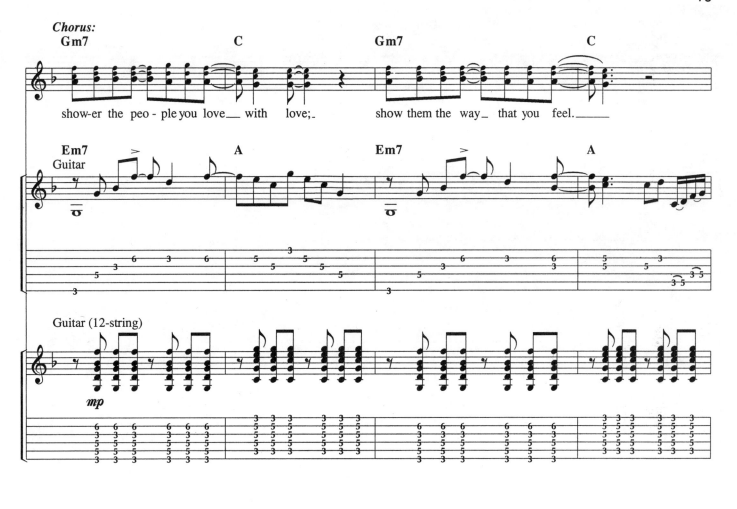

show-er the peo - ple you love__ with love;__ show them the way__ that you feel._____

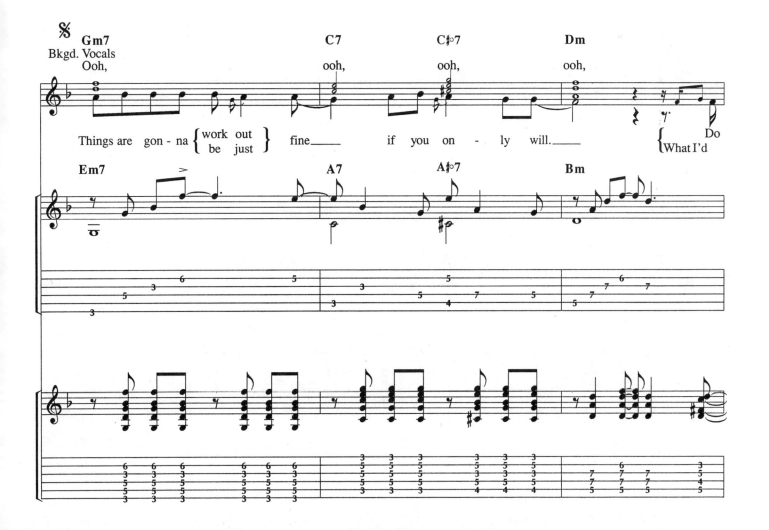

Things are gon - na {work out / be just} fine____ if you on - ly will.____ {Do / What I'd

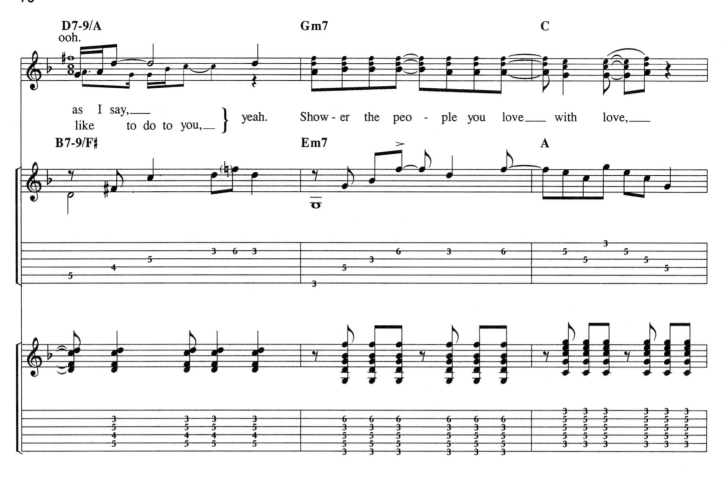

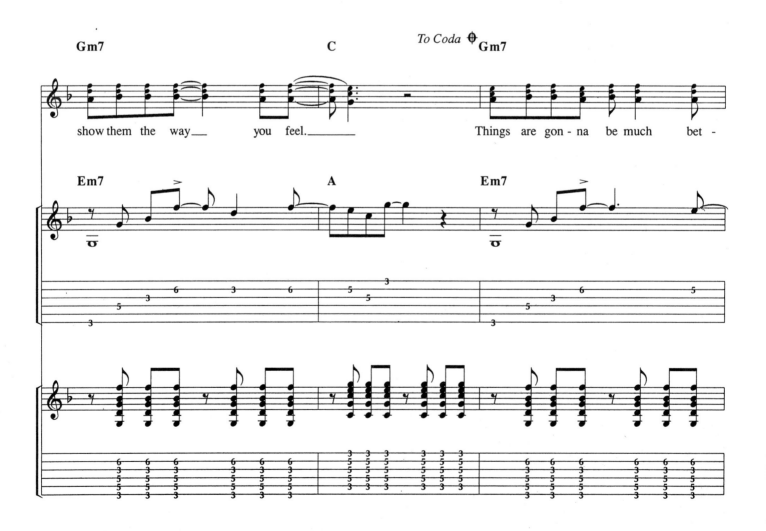

Played by Bass.

Additional Lyrics

Ad lib. Vocal: They say in every life,   Love is sunshine.
They say the rain must fall.   Love, love love is sunshine.
Just like the pouring rain,   Make it rain
Make it rain.   Love, love love is sunshine. Alright, yeah.
Everybody, everybody, everybody, everybody.

Sweet Baby James

Words and Music by
JAMES TAYLOR

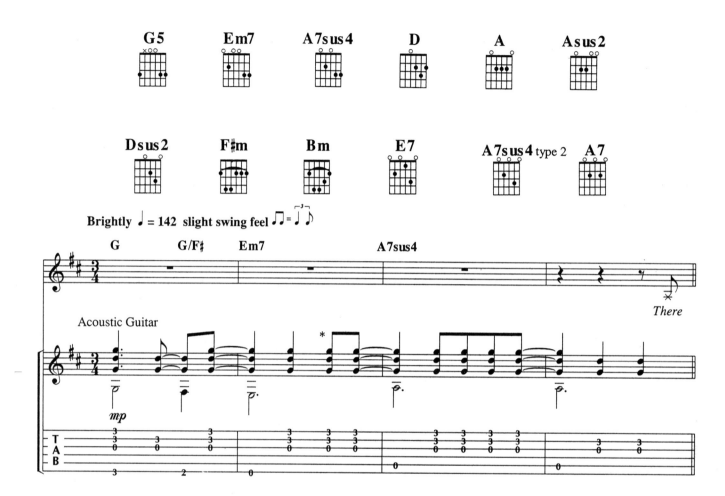

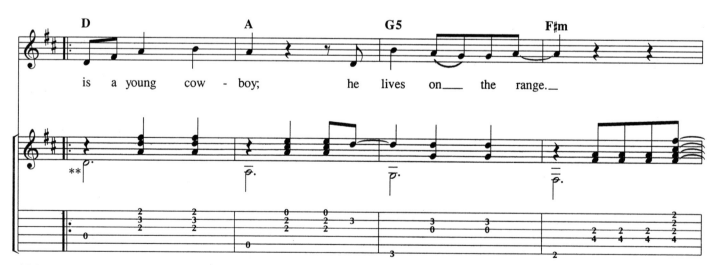

*8th note rhythms can be strummed with fingers or thumb.
**2nd Verse – ad lib. on 1st Verse line.

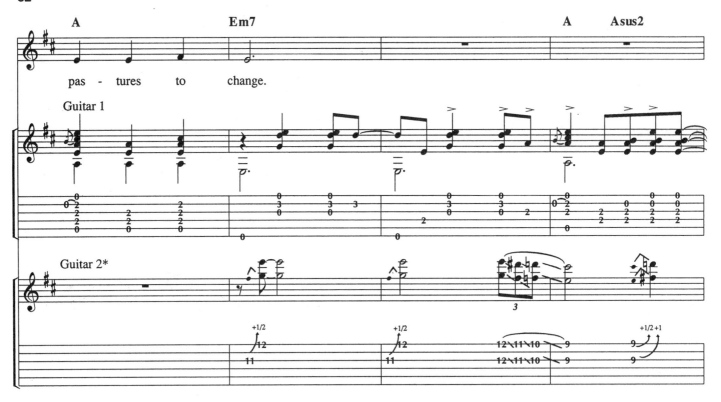

pas - tures   to   change.

Guitar 1

Guitar 2*

And   as   the   moon   ris - es   he   sits   by   his   fire,___

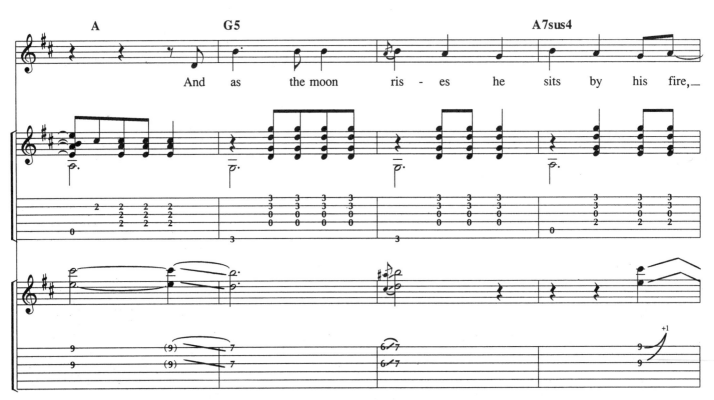

Pedal Steel arranged for Guitar.

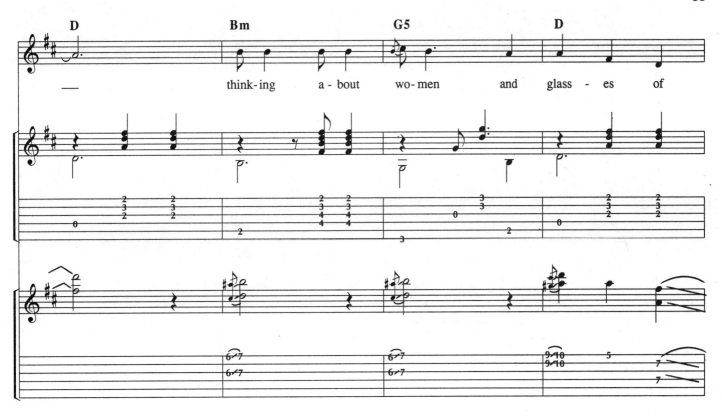

think-ing a - bout wo-men and glass-es of

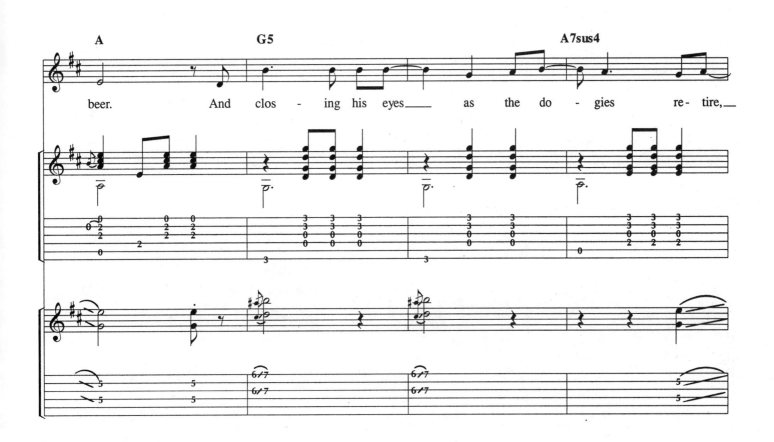

beer. And clos - ing his eyes___ as the do - gies re - tire,___

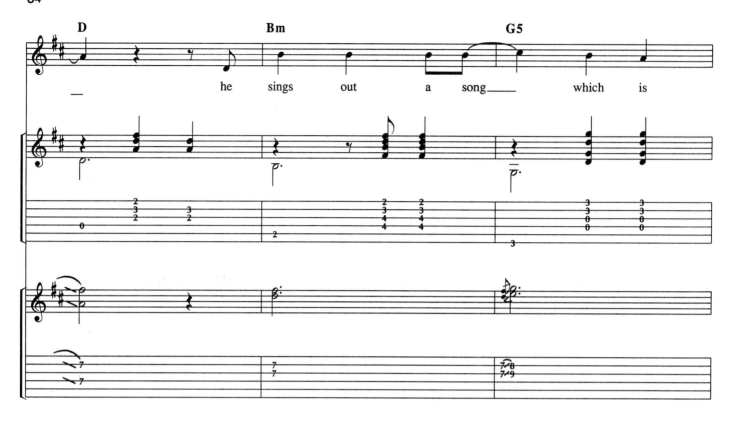

he sings out a song___ which is

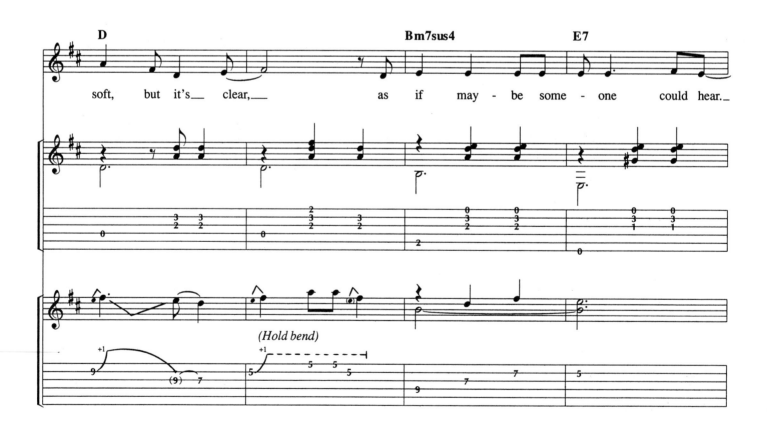

soft, but it's___ clear,___ as if may - be some - one could hear.___

(Hold bend)

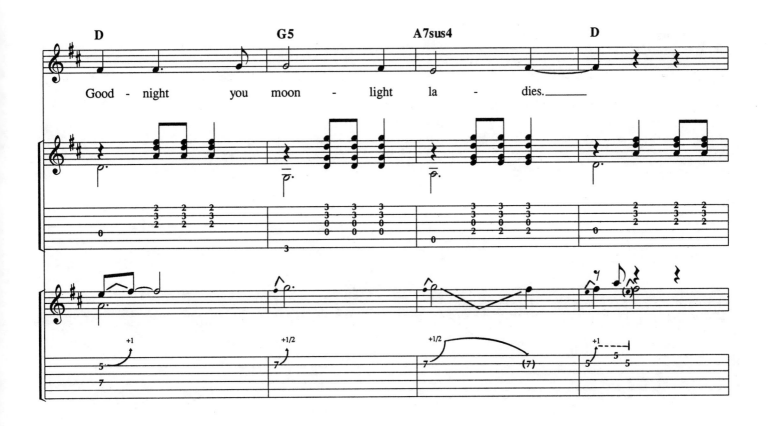

Good - night   you   moon - light   la -   dies.____

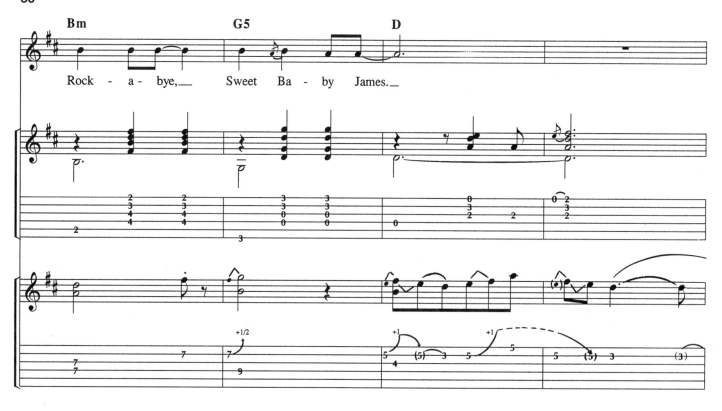

Rock - a - bye,___ Sweet Ba - by James.___

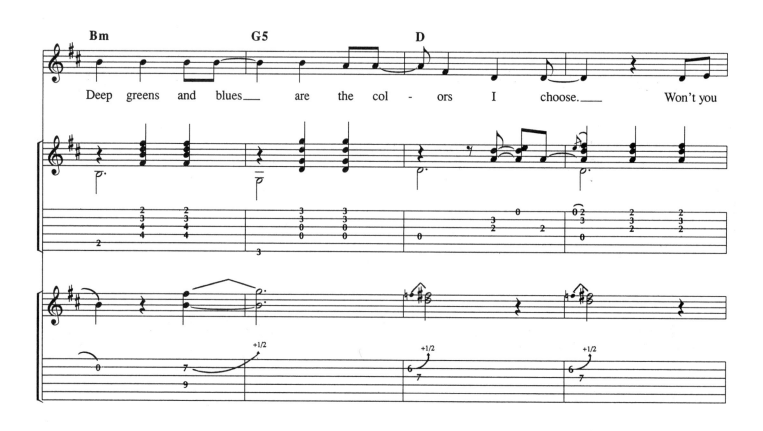

Deep greens and blues___ are the col - ors I choose.___ Won't you

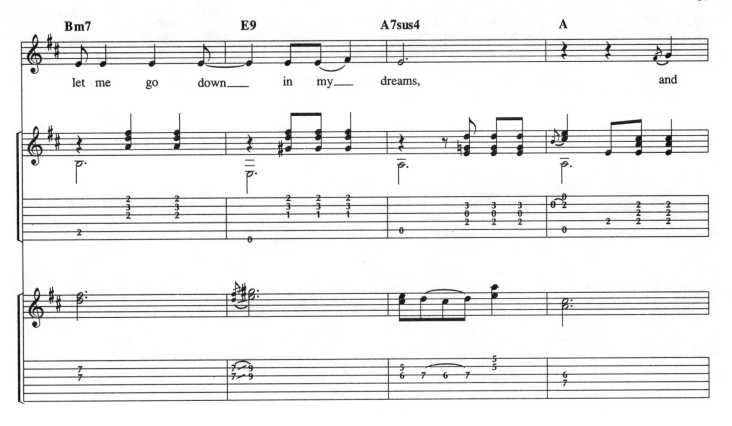

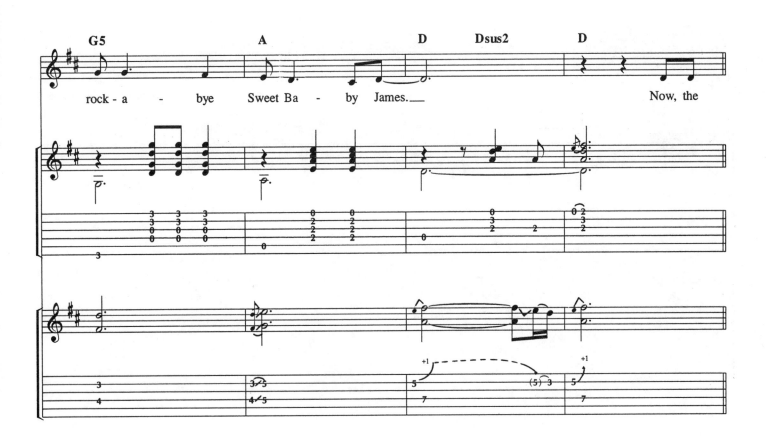

first of De-cem - ber was cov - ered with snow.

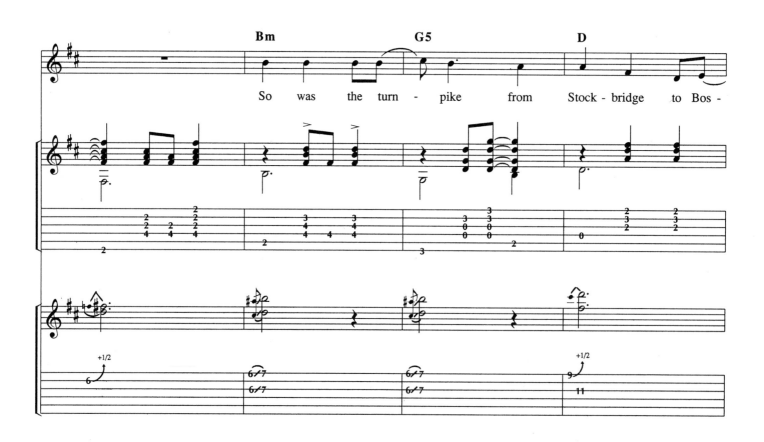

So was the turn - pike from Stock - bridge to Bos -

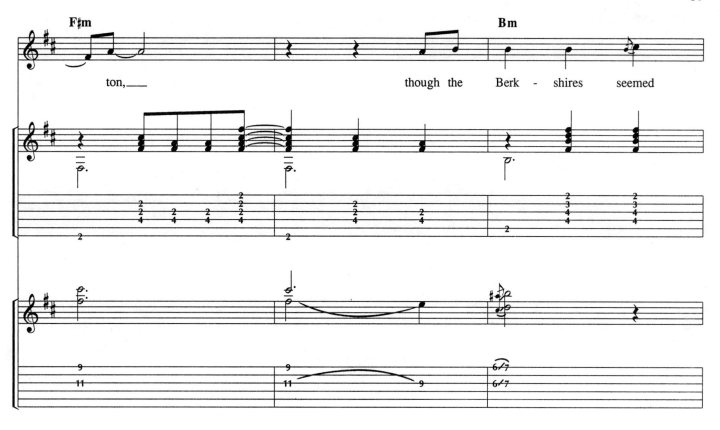

ton,_____ though the Berk - shires seemed

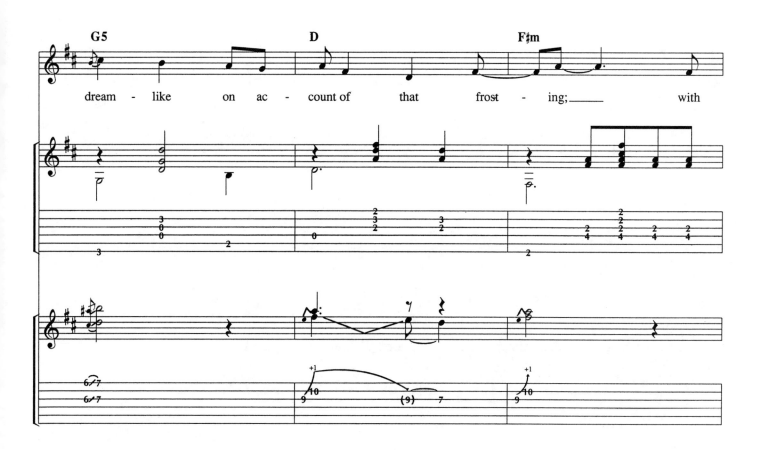

dream - like on ac - count of that frost - ing;_____ with

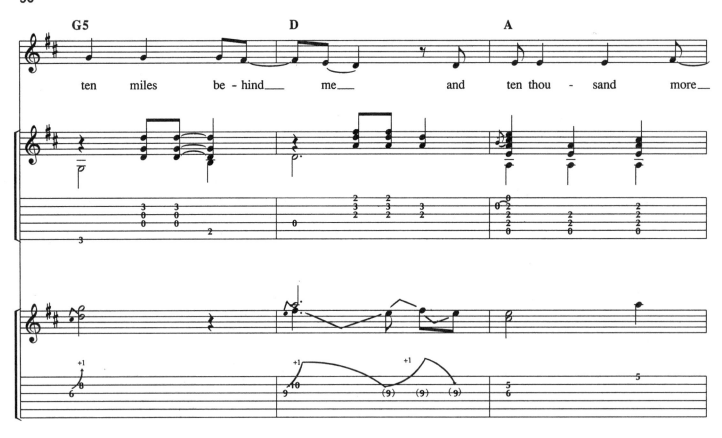

ten   miles   be - hind___ me___   and ten thou - sand   more___

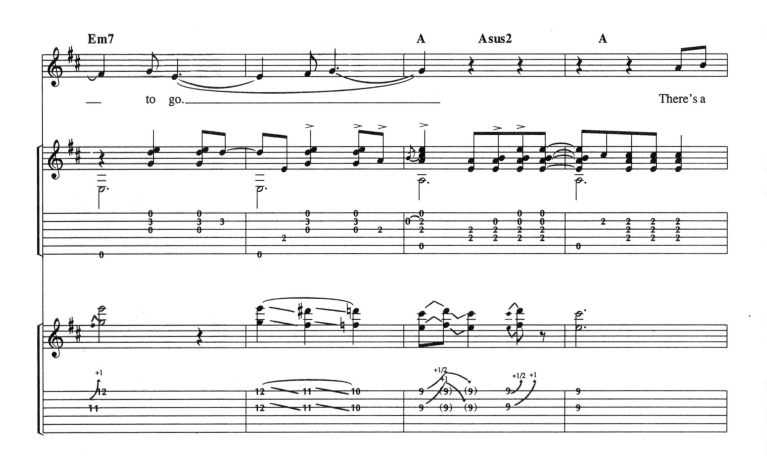

___   to   go._____   There's a

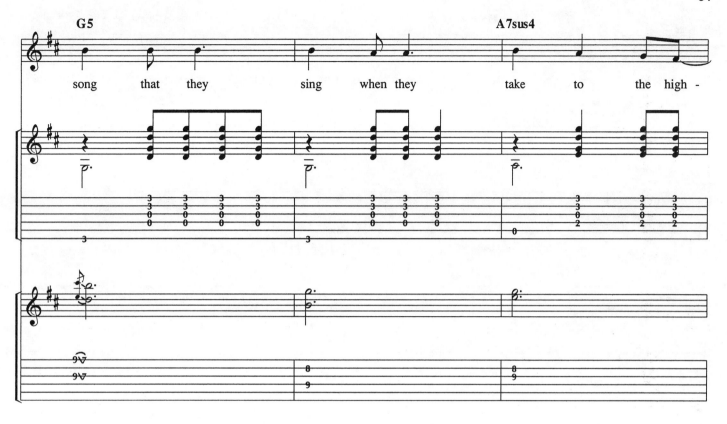

song that they sing when they take to the high-

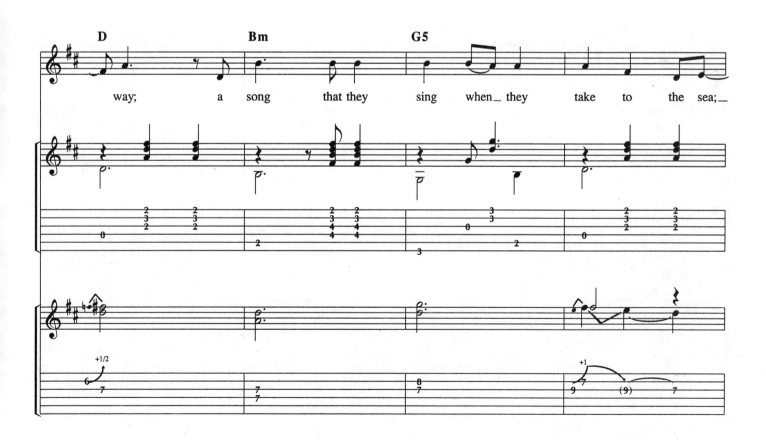

way; a song that they sing when they take to the sea;

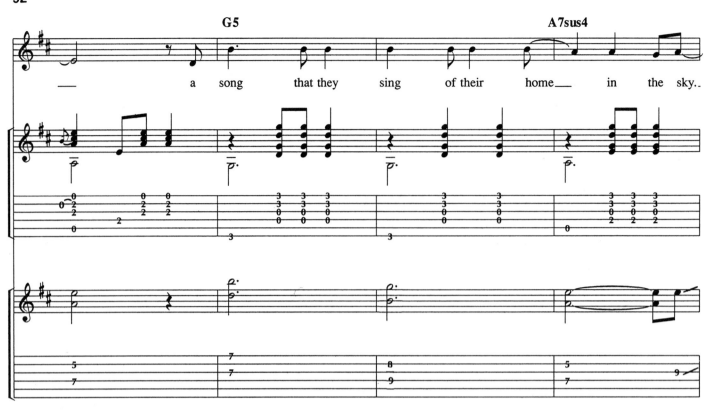

a song that they sing of their home___ in the sky..

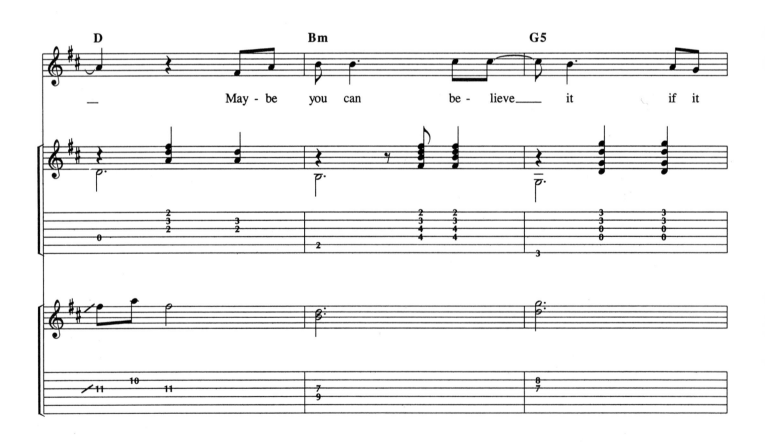

May - be you can be - lieve___ it if it

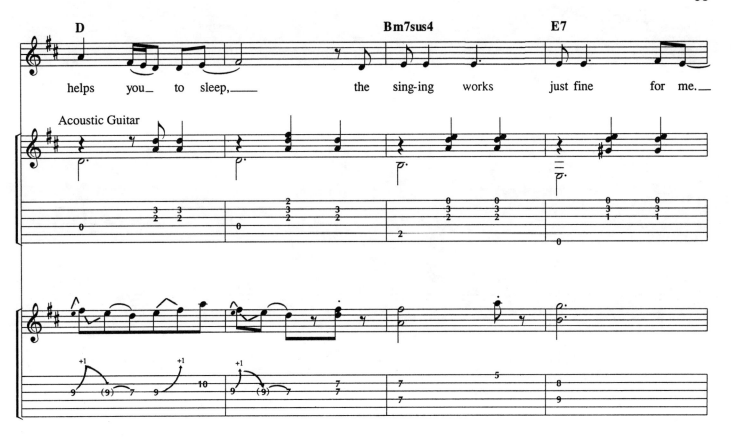

helps   you__ to sleep,____   the sing-ing works   just fine   for me.__

Acoustic Guitar

_____ So__

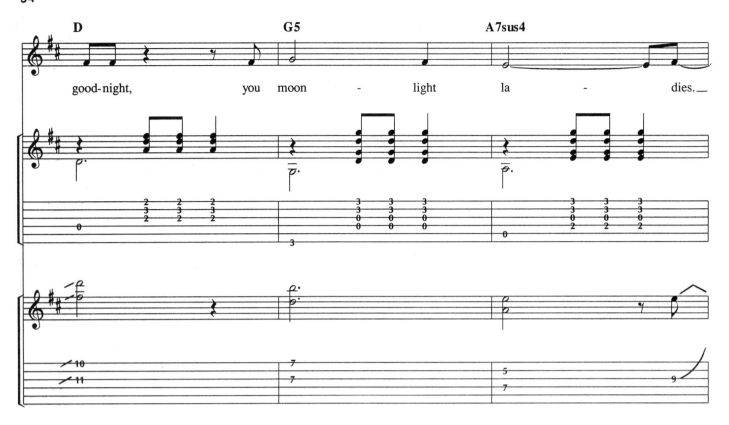

good-night, you moon - light la - dies.

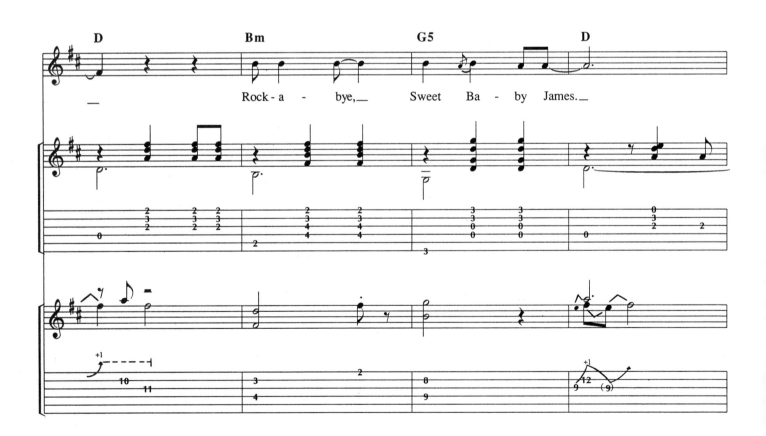

Rock - a - bye,__ Sweet Ba - by James.__

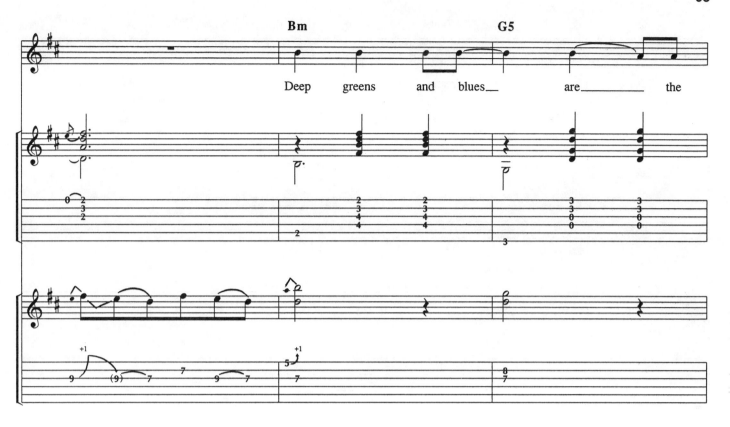

Deep greens and blues___ are_____ the

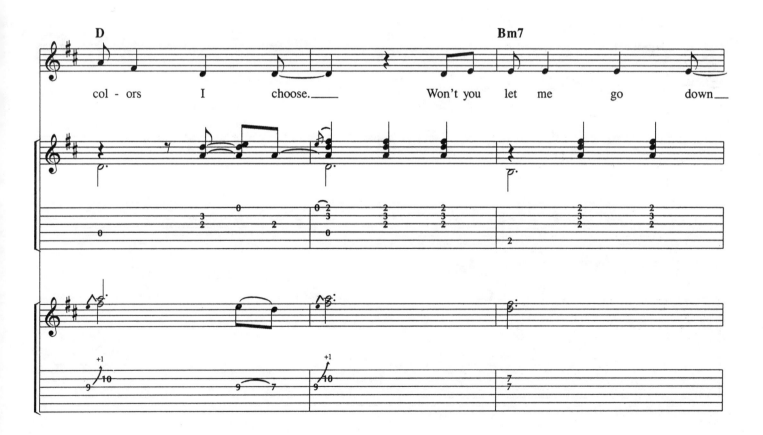

col - ors I choose.___ Won't you let me go down___

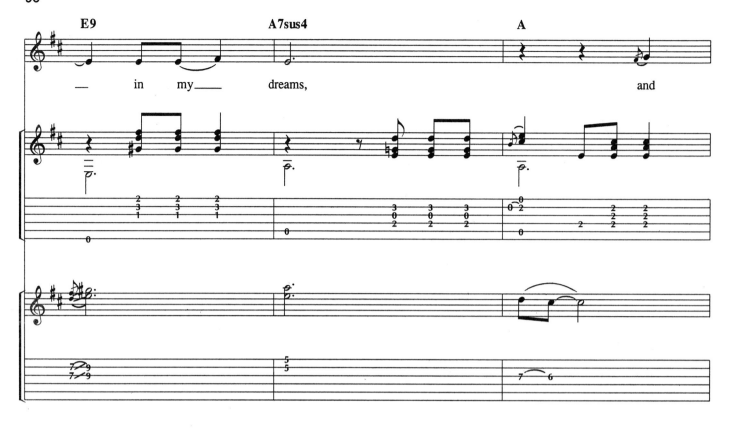

in my dreams, and

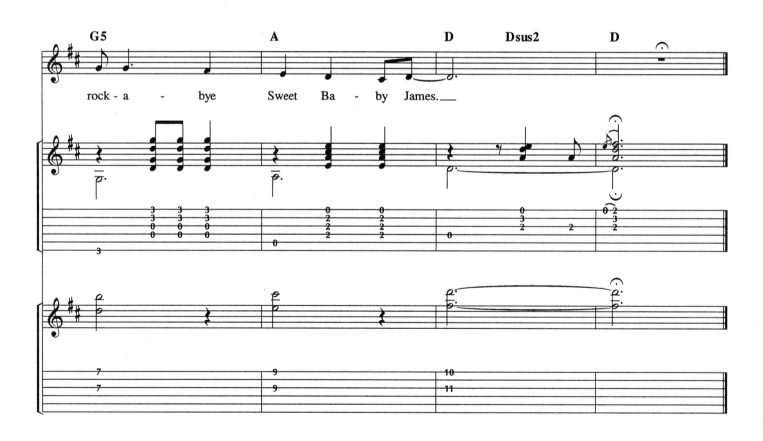

rock - a - bye Sweet Ba - by James.

Walking Man

Words and Music by
JAMES TAYLOR

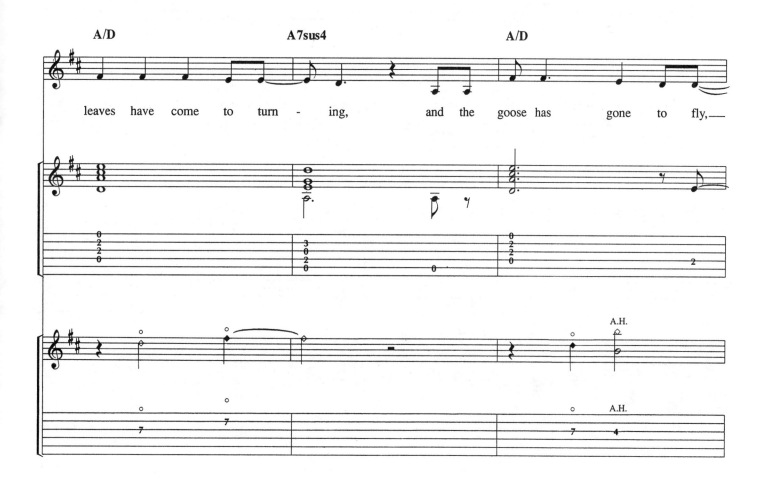

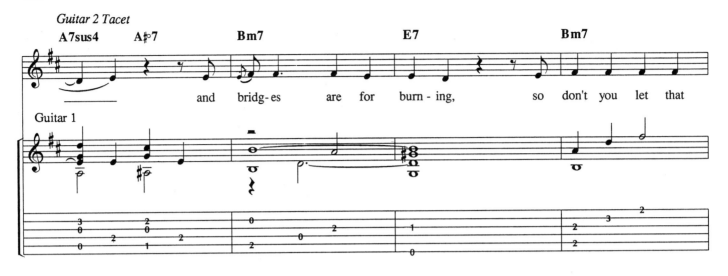

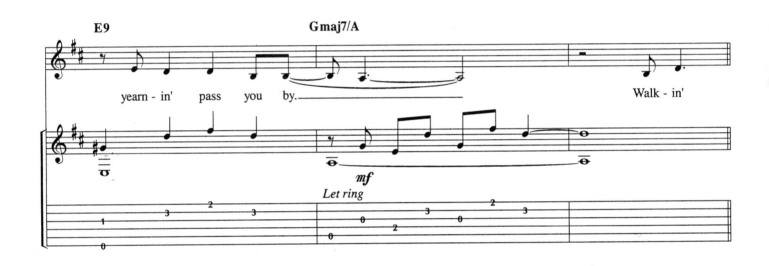

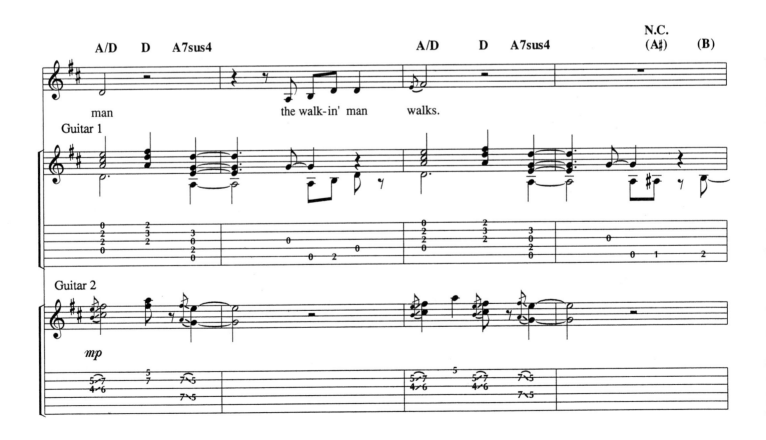

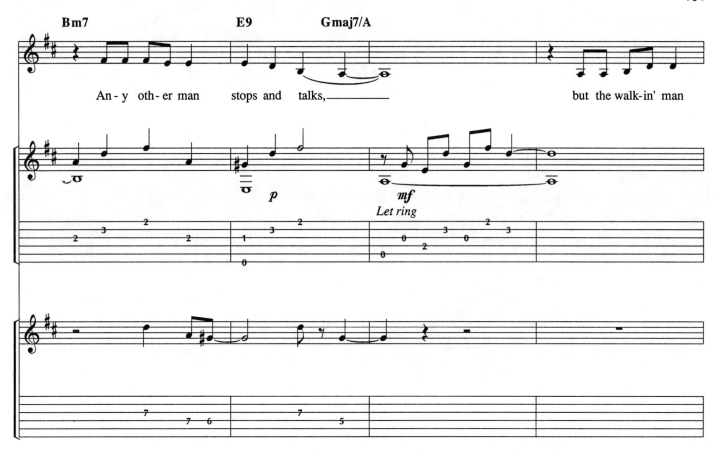

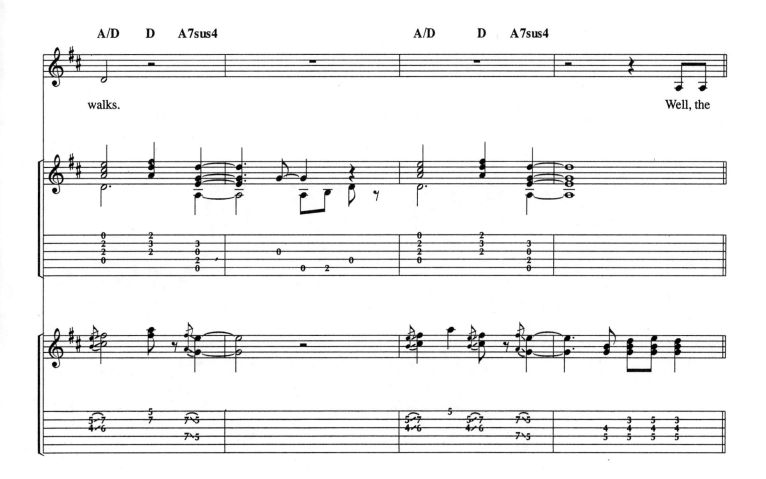

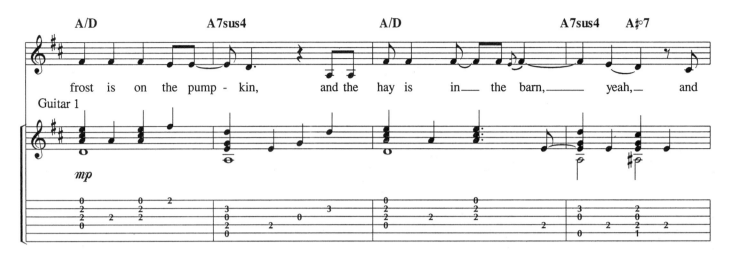

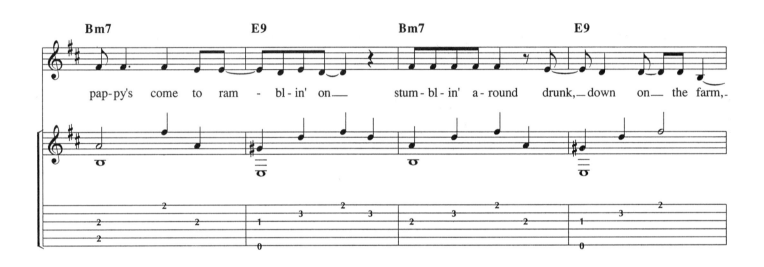

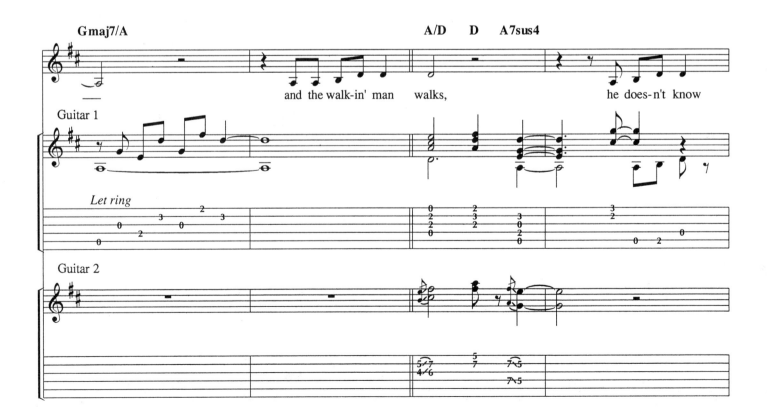

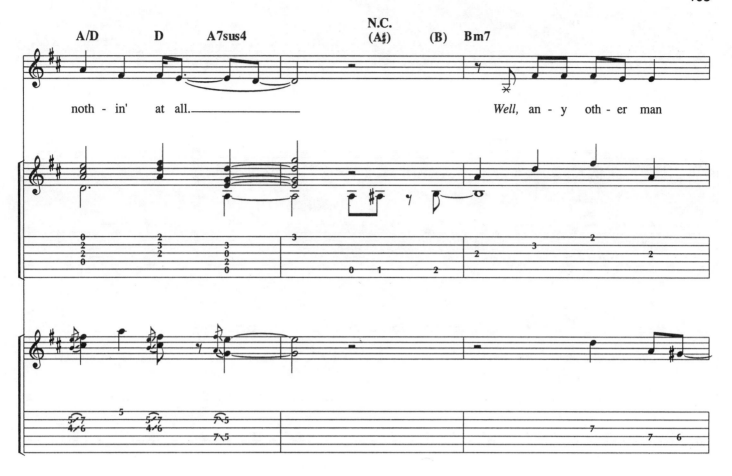

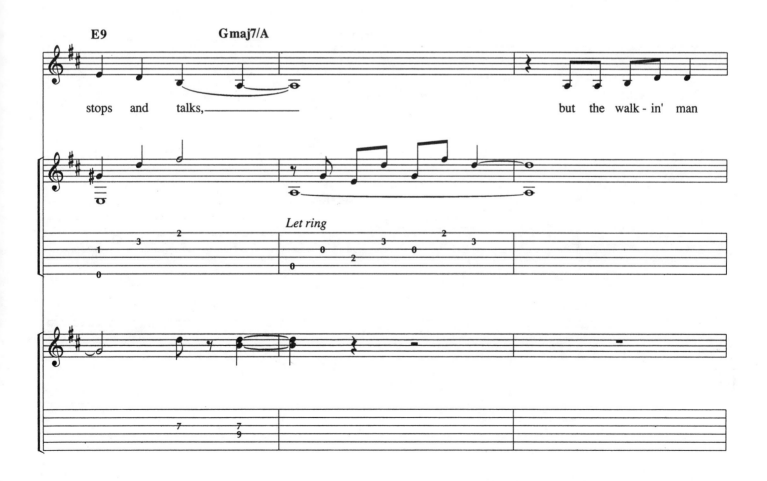

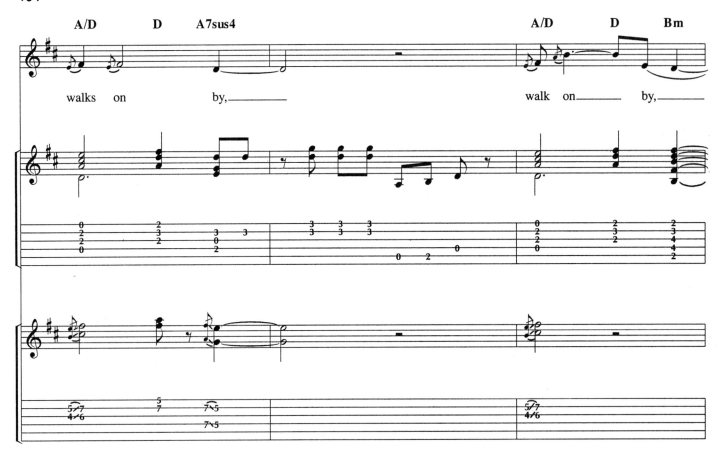

walks on by,———— walk on———— by,————

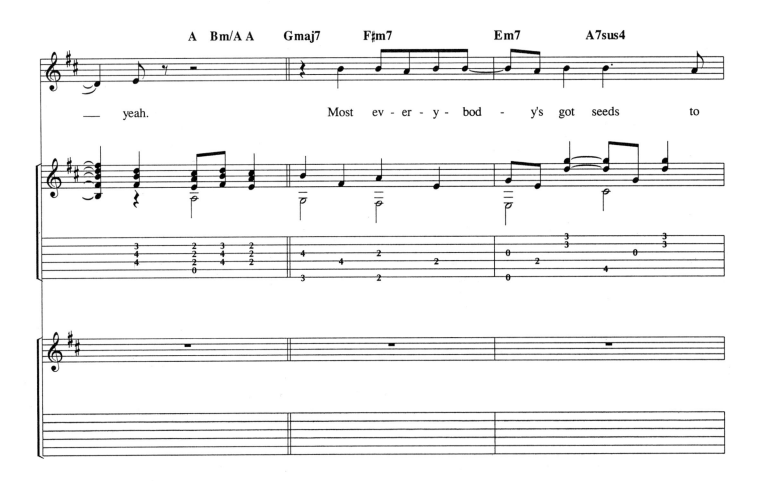

— yeah. Most ev - er - y - bod - y's got seeds to

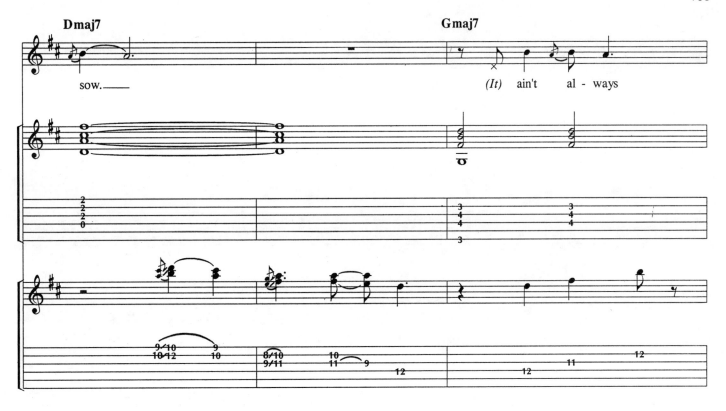

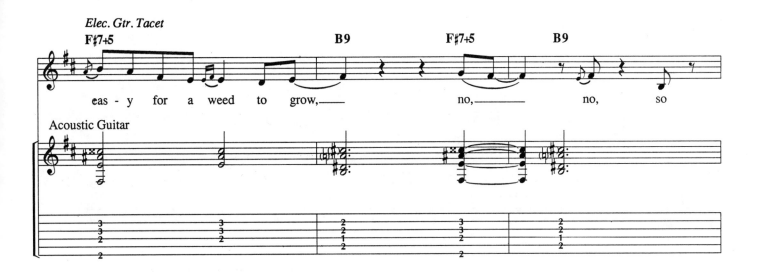

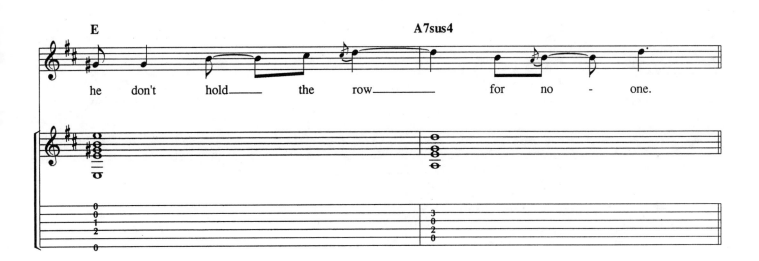

Acoustic Guitar overdub.

You Can Close Your Eyes

Words and Music by
JAMES TAYLOR

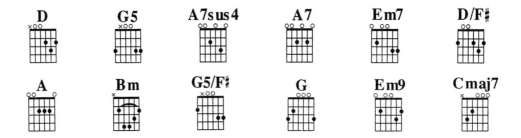

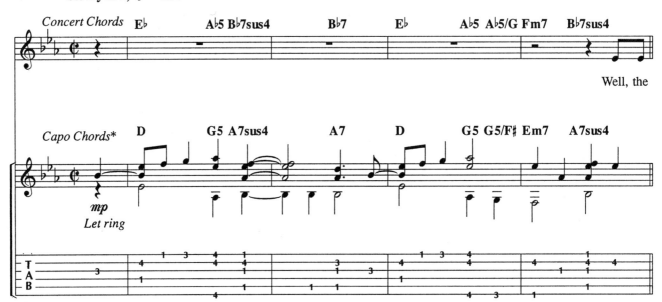

*Capo at 1st fret.

* Without capo

* *Without capo*

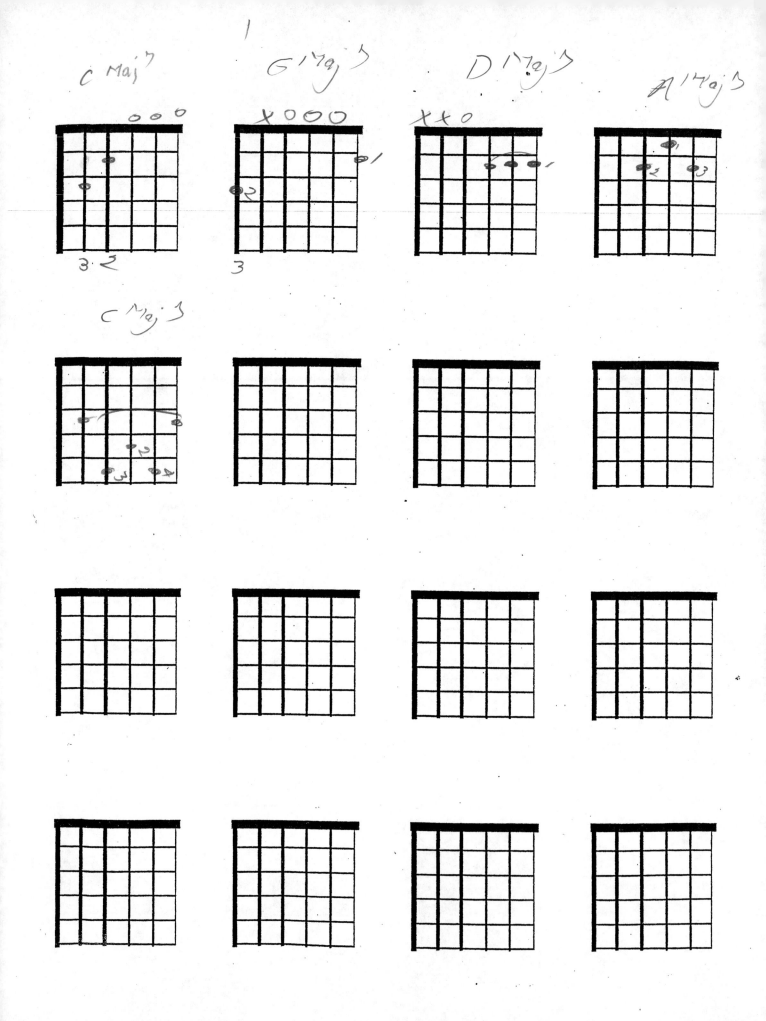

You've Got A Friend

Words and Music by
CAROLE KING

*Capo on 2nd fret.

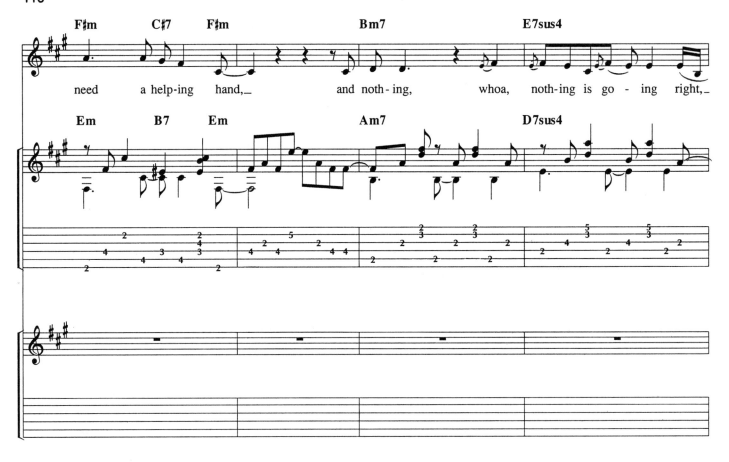

need a help-ing hand,___ and noth-ing, whoa, noth-ing is go - ing right,___

close you're eyes___ and think of me and

soon I will_ be there___ to bright-en up

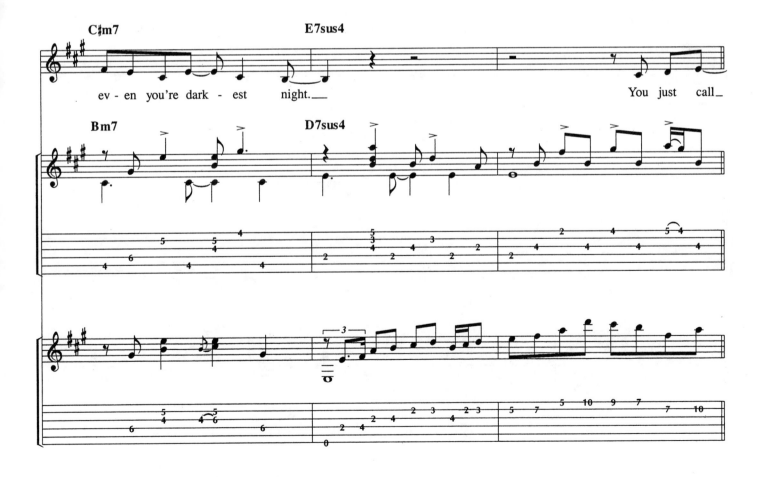

ev-en you're dark-est night.___ You just call_

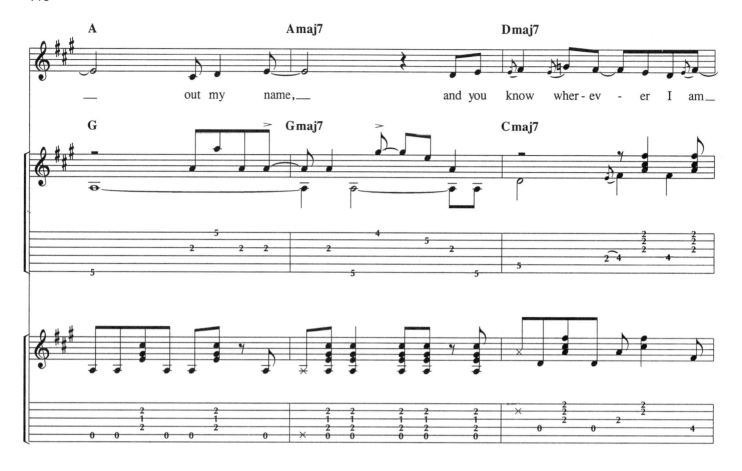

out my name,___ and you know wher-ev - er I am___

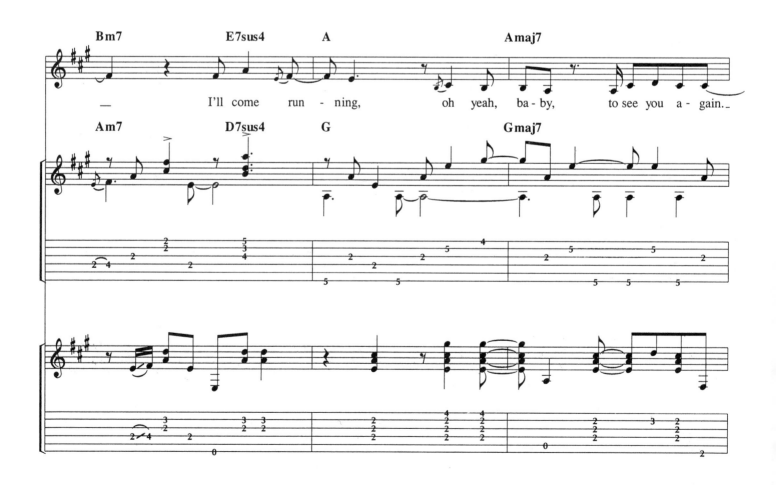

I'll come run - ning, oh yeah, ba - by, to see you a - gain.___

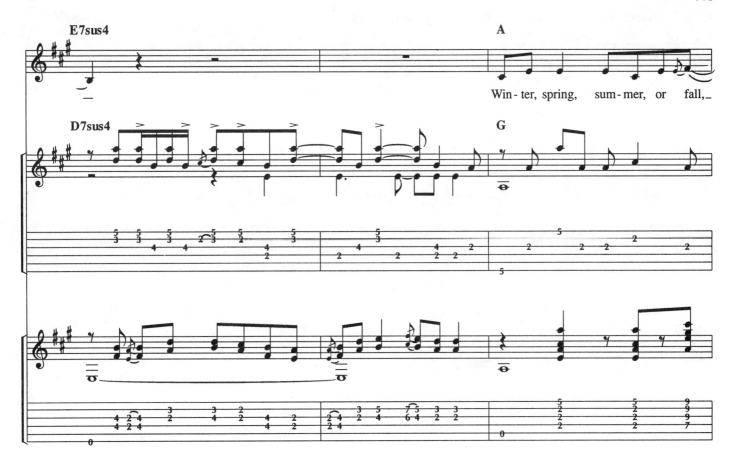

Win - ter, spring, sum - mer, or fall,_

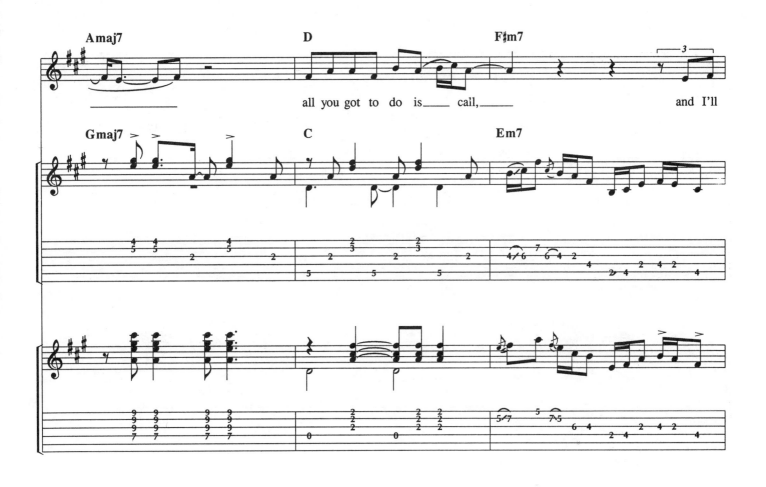

all you got to do is___ call,_____ and I'll

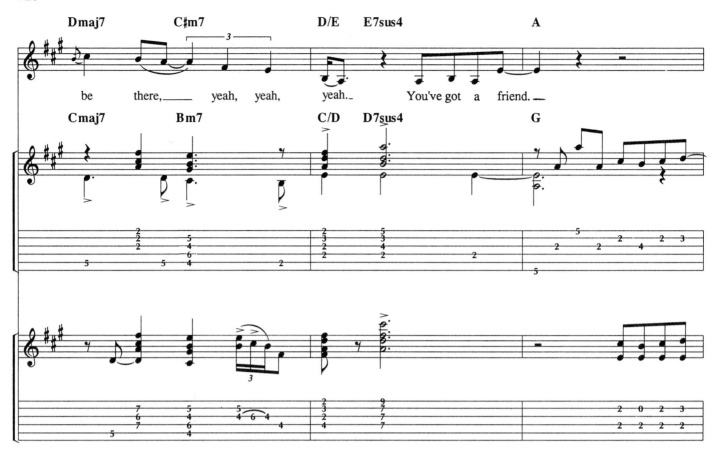

be there,_____ yeah, yeah, yeah.__ You've got a friend.__

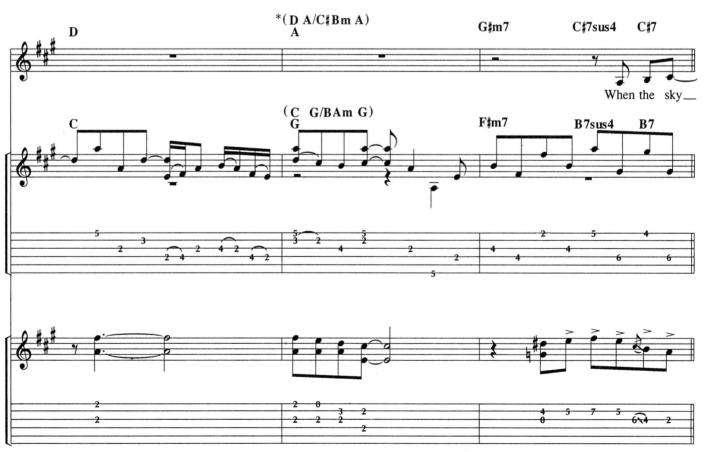

When the sky__

Harmony implied by Bass.

a - bove___ you should turn___ dark___ and full of clouds,___

and that old north wind___ should be - gin to blow,___

keep your head__ to - geth - er and

call my name_____ out__ loud,_____ now. Soon I'll be knock-

in'___ up-on your door.___ You just call___

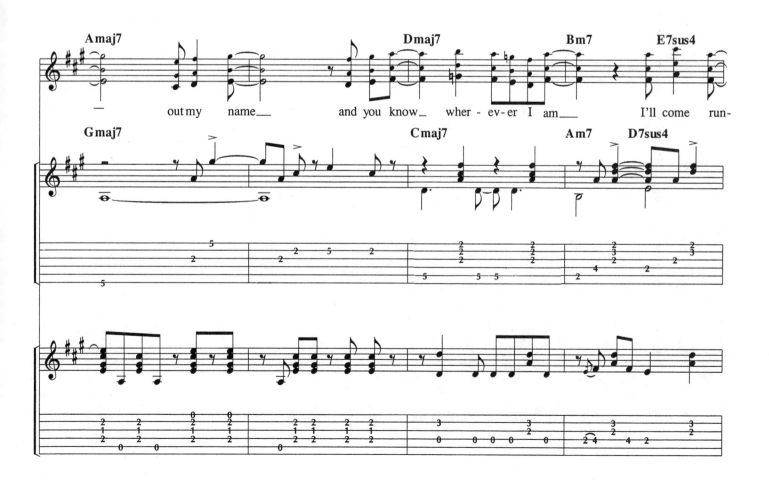

out my name___ and you know___ wher-ev-er I am___ I'll come run-

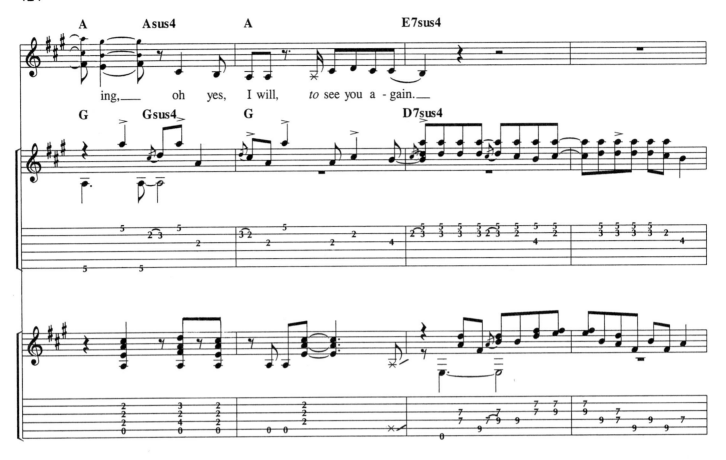

ing,___ oh yes, I will, *to* see you a - gain.___

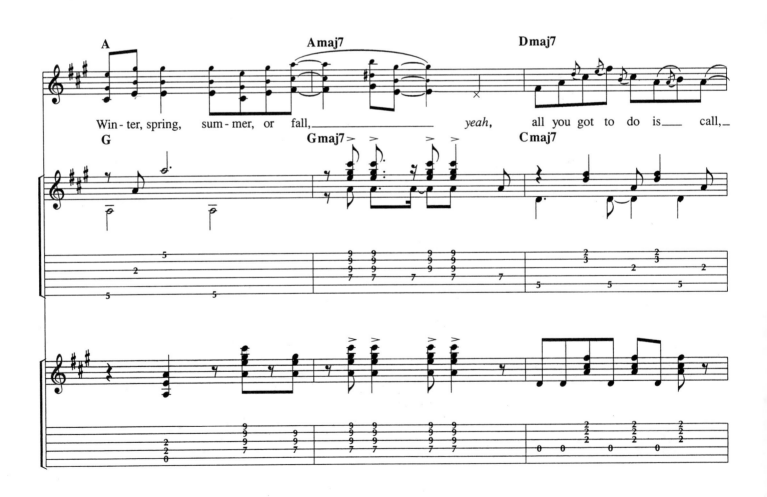

Win - ter, spring, sum - mer, or fall,_____ *yeah,* all you got to do is___ call,___

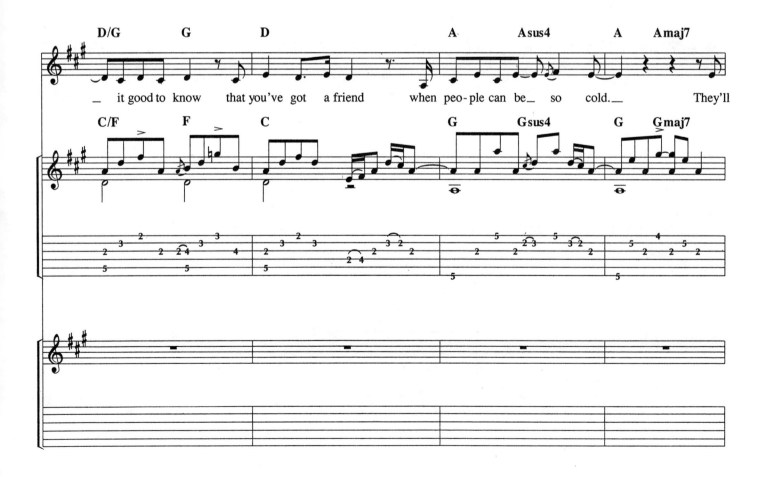

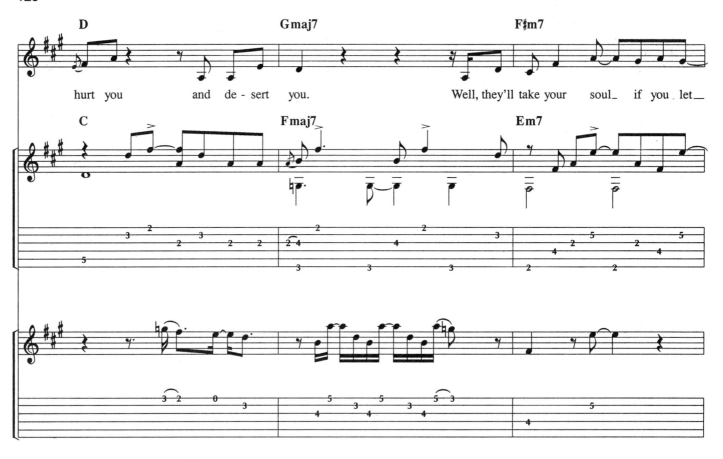

hurt you   and de-sert you.   Well, they'll take your   soul_ if you _ let_

_ them.   Oh,   yeah, but don't_ you   let them.   You just   call___   out my   name,_

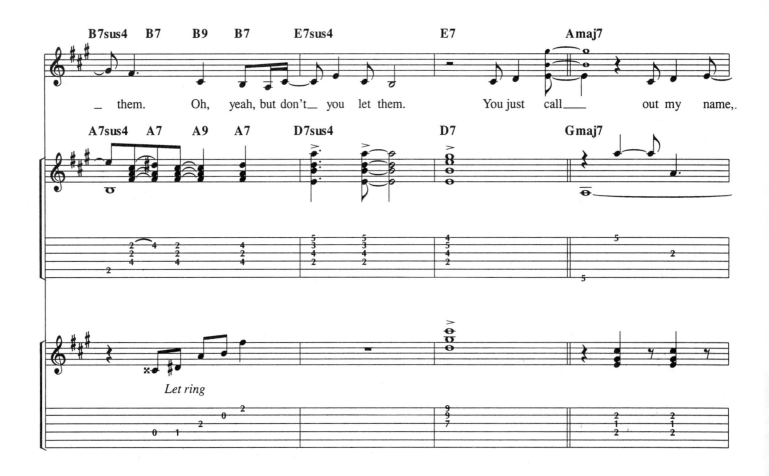

Let ring

and you know wher- ev - er I am,___ I'll come run - ning___

out my name

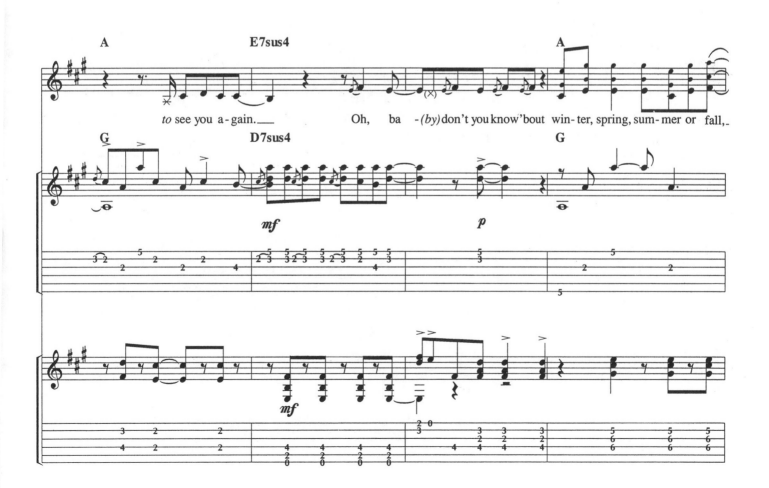

to see you a - gain.___ Oh, ba -(by) don't you know 'bout win - ter, spring, sum - mer or fall,_